Arty Facts

Communication
& Art Activities

Crabtree Publishing Company

www.crabtreebooks.com

Crabtree Publishing Company

PMB 16A, 350 Fifth Avenue, Suite 3308
New York, NY
10118

612 Welland Avenue
St. Catharines, Ontario
L2M 5V6

Coordinating Editor: Ellen Rodger

Project Editor: Carrie Gleason

Production Coordinator: Rosie Gowsell

Project Development and Concept Marshall Direct:
Editorial Project Director: Karen Foster
Editors: Claire Sippi, Hazel Songhurst, Samantha Sweeney
Researchers: Gerry Bailey, Alec Edgington
Design Director: Tracy Carrington
Designers: Flora Awolaja, Claire Penny, Paul Montague,
James Thompson, Mark Dempsey,
Production: Victoria Grimsell, Christina Brown
Photo Research: Andrea Sadler
Illustrator: Jan Smith
Model Artist: Sophie Dean

Prepress, printing, and binding by Worzalla Publishing Company

Stringer, John, 1934-
    Communication and art activities / written by John Stringer.
        p. cm. -- (Arty facts)
    Includes index.
    Summary: Provides information about the many forms of human communication
throughout history and accompanying craft projects.
    ISBN 0-7787-1119-6 (RLB) -- ISBN 0-7787-1147-1 (PB)
    1. Communication--Juvenile literature.   [1. Communication. 2. Handicraft.]
I. Title. II. Series.
    P91.2.S77 2003
    302.2--dc21
                                                                2002011588
                                                                LC

Created by
Marshall Direct Learning

© 2002 Marshall Direct Learning

FRONT COVER IMAGES: MARY JELLIFFE/ ANCIENT ART & ARCHITECTURE COLLECTION; GEOFF TOMPKINSON/ SCIENCE PHOTO LIBRARY; THE HUTCHISON LIBRARY; DAMIEN LOVEGROVE/ SCIENCE PHOTO LIBRARY

Linking art to the world around us

Arty Facts

Communication
& Art Activities

Contents

WRITTEN BY John Stringer

Rows of beads

Imagine you are at a market in ancient Egypt. You spot a weary merchant who has traveled from far away to sell perfumes, silk, and spices. As the merchant sells his goods to a customer, he keeps track of the cost by quickly sliding beads across rows on a wooden instrument. He counts faster than if he were using a modern calculator! The wooden counting machine the merchant is using is called an **abacus**.

This man in a Hong Kong market makes and repairs modern-day abacuses.

International adding machine

The abacus was invented by people in different parts of the world at the same time. The ancient Egyptians, the **Babylonians**, and the Chinese were using abacuses 5,000 years ago. When the Spanish first reached Central America in the late 1400s, they found the **Mayan** people using the abacus too.

Speed counting

The beads in each row of an abacus represent numbers. In a base-ten abacus, there is a row for counting ones, a row for counting tens, a row for counting hundreds, and so on. The beads are pushed along the rows to add numbers.

Counting frame

WHAT YOU NEED

small cardboard box

air-drying clay

string

glitter

paints and brush

knitting needle

1

Decorate your box with colored paints. Use the knitting needle to poke three holes, one above the other, in each side of the box, as shown.

2

Roll small pieces of clay into 30 round balls. Push the knitting needle through the middle of each clay ball to make a hole. Leave to harden.

3

Paint the balls and decorate with glitter.

Use your abacus to count ones on the bottom row, tens on the middle row, and hundreds on the top row.

4

Thread one piece of string through each hole on one side of the box. Knot the strings on the outside of the box. Thread ten clay balls onto each piece of string.

5

Push the free ends of the strings through the holes on the other side of the box and tie firmly.

Use your abacus to make high-speed calculations

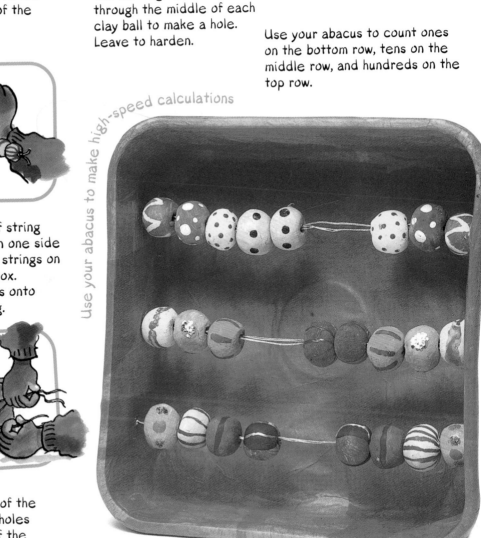

5

Flying flags

A flag is usually a rectangular piece of cloth with a special design on it. A flag is an **emblem** for a person, a country, or an organization. All nations, and many states, towns, and cities, have their own flags. Organizations such as Boy Scouts and the Red Cross also have their own flags. Flags are used to send messages and give information.

First flags

In ancient Egypt, flag-like objects appeared in wall paintings. These paintings consisted of symbols on top of lines, or poles. The first cloth flags were used in China around 3000 B.C. and were made of silk. During the **Middle Ages** in Europe, soldiers called knights carried square flags with long streamers.

A knight who was promoted to a higher position had this flag cut off and replaced with a new flag called a banner. These higher-ranking knights were called bannerets.

Flag colors

There are seven basic colors generally used in national flags: red, white, green, orange, black, yellow, and blue.

Flags at sea

Ships at sea used flags to send messages to other ships or to shore before there was radio **communication**. Ships carried a large number of flags with different designs. Crew members signaled other ships using a combination of flags. Ships salute one another at sea by lowering, or dipping, their flag.

Bright banners

Hang your banner of flags to brighten up a party or special occasion

colored paper

scissors

string

gluestick

white paper

paints

pencil

paintbrush

1 Cut triangular and square shapes out of colored and patterned paper.

2 Fold the shapes in half and glue them to a piece of string.

3 On white paper, draw and paint some simple pictures to fit on the flags.

4 Cut out the pictures and glue them onto the flags.

Knots for counting

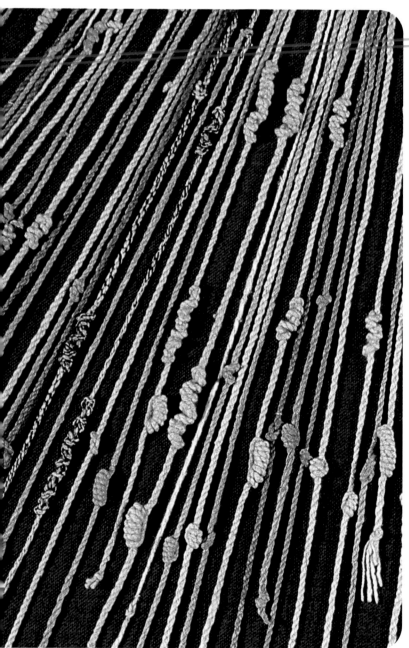

Knots are used for tying up many different things, including shoes, boxes, and boats. Knots have other uses too. They can even be used for counting!

Measuring with string

The Inca people of South America tied knots in strings of different lengths and colors. The knots were used for counting and keeping records of amounts. The Incas called these knotted strings quipus. The colors of the strings and the size and location of the knots all represented different numbers.

Log chip and line

Knots were once used on ships to measure how fast they were traveling. Every ship carried a measuring device called a log chip and line. The line was wound around a reel and the chip, or piece of wood, was dragged in the water behind the ship. As the ship moved along, the line unwound.

How many knots?

The line had knots tied in it every 47 feet (14.4 m). For example, at 47 feet (14.4 m) one knot was tied, at 94 feet (28.8 m) two knots were tied, and so on. Sailors let the line unwind for 28 seconds behind the ship. At the end of the 28 seconds, sailors stopped the line from unwinding and noted the number of knots at that point. If the line had unwound to the five knot mark, then the ship was moving at a speed of five knots, or five nautical miles per hour.

Mississippi marks

Steamboats on the Mississippi River used ropes with knots in them to measure the depth of the river, to make sure it was not too shallow for the boats. Each knot was called a "mark." A depth of two knots, called a "mark twain," was 12 feet (3.7 m), a safe depth for the boats.

Communication

Quipu curtain

Hang your quipu on your wall, in a doorway, or at a window

string

scissors

beads

bamboo stick

1 Cut eight equal pieces of string and tie them to the bamboo stick.

2 Knot together each pair of strings, moving along the row. Then repeat, knotting alternate strings together.

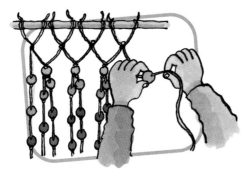

3 Thread a bead onto each piece of string. Tie knots to hold the beads. Add as many beads and knots as you like to all the strings.

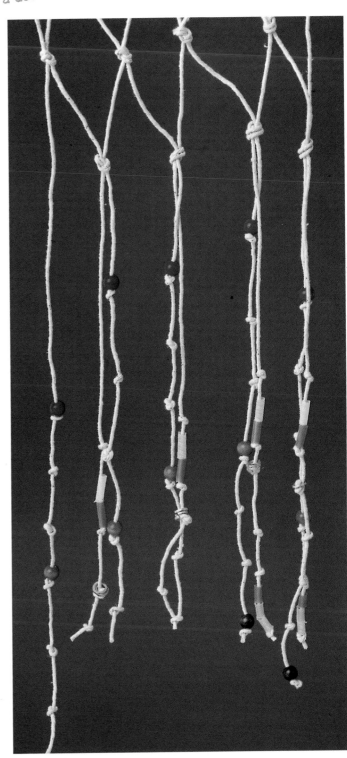

Signs and symbols

Before alphabets and writing were invented, people told stories, sent messages, or kept lists using symbols and pictures. Ancient Egyptians used a system of written communication made up of pictures instead of words. Each picture, called a hieroglyph, was a sign that stood for a name, a place, or an object. Hieroglyphs took a long time to write. There are no periods, commas, or sentences in hieroglyphs, so it is hard to tell where to start reading and where to stop!

Scratches on clay

The first people to write lived in Sumer, in what is now part of the modern country of Iraq, 10,000 years ago. They scratched simple pictures on clay **tablets** to help them remember details about their land, animals, and crops.

Sounds system

The biggest step in the story of writing was the use of symbols for spoken sounds instead of just for objects and ideas. This made writing easier, because the writers, or scribes, only had to learn the symbol for each sound. Over time, the symbols slowly developed into the letters of our modern alphabets.

The background picture shows ancient Egyptian hieroglyphs. Historians could not read hieroglyphs until the Rosetta stone (front) was found. The Rosetta stone uses two different languages and three different types of writing, including hieroglyphs.

Calligraphic art

tea bags

white construction paper

thin paintbrush

black paint

paints and brush

pencil

poster board

1 Brush cold black tea on both sides of the construction paper with a paintbrush.

2 After the paper is dry, draw imaginary Japanese, Chinese, or Arabic characters in pencil.

4 Finish the painting with an imaginary red seal and signature.

5 Mount on colored poster board.

3 Use the thin paintbrush to paint over the characters with watery black paint.

Design your own symbol or character alphabet and write secret messages to your friends

11

Smoke and drums

People sent information over long distances by much simpler methods before there was telephone and **e-mail**. Sometimes communicating involved sending signals that could be interpreted as words or ideas. Two of the earliest ways to send signals were by beating a drum and by creating puffs of smoke. Drums can be heard over long distances, and smoke can be seen from far away.

Drum messages

The first drums were made of animal skin stretched over hollow logs. The booming noise the drums made when struck was used to send messages quickly over a long distance. Only simple messages, such as a warning, could be sent. Drum signals were used by Native North Americans and by many African and Asian peoples.

Puffs of smoke

One way to make smoke signals is by lighting a fire with green wood, which makes plenty of smoke. North American Native peoples held blankets over fires to hold down the smoke, then let it rise into the sky in a special way. The number of puffs and the delay between puffs were interpreted by other members of the group. Smoke signals were an effective way of signaling danger, such as warning that an enemy was approaching. Signals were also used to tell others about good hunting, such as the location of a herd of buffalo.

Talking drum

WHAT YOU NEED

plastic container with lid

tissue paper

sequins

glitter

gluestick

paints and brush

1 Glue strips of colored tissue paper onto your container so that it is covered all over.

2 Decorate it with sequins, beads, buttons, and other materials.

3 Paint the lid a bright color and leave to dry.

Make different sounds by putting pebbles or sand inside the container. Now you can shake your drum as well.

Codes and ciphers

Secret messages are sent in code. Codes are symbols or groups of letters used to represent words. A cipher is a code in which letters have been replaced by other letters, numbers, or symbols. For example, if you replace each letter of the alphabet with the next letter, a message saying: "IFSF JT B TFDSFU" means "Here is a secret".

Caesar's code

Ciphers are useful for keeping information from an enemy. The Roman leader Julius Caesar used one of the first ciphers. He replaced each letter in a message with another letter three places further along in the alphabet. To read, or decipher, the message, a **cipher disk** was used. The outer disk was turned to line up a letter in the secret message with a letter on the inner disk. Each letter of the code was then replaced by the correct letter, and the message was read.

Speedy messages

Morse code is a code that uses long and short light and sound signals, or printed dots and dashes. Each signal represents a letter of the alphabet. The best known signal in Morse code is . . . – – – . . . This means SOS and is an international signal for emergencies.

Cracking codes

Code breakers are people who decipher how a code works. Most codes and ciphers based on scrambled letters are easy to break. In English, some letters are used more than others. You write a lot more Es than you do Zs! Code breakers start by counting letters until they figure out the Es and As, then they can crack the rest of the code. Some codes use a secret key, such as a word or a number that changes with every new message. E-mail messages are also sent in code. First, a **public key** scrambles the message so that it cannot be read by anyone else. When it arrives, a secret **private key** unscrambles it.

A bar code is printed on things we buy. It has eleven bars which stand for the product, the maker, the color, weight, and size. In the store, a laser scanner decodes each stripe at the checkout.

Dial-a-code

WHAT YOU NEED

painted cardboard

glitter glue

two plates

pencil

gluestick

black and silver pens

gold glitter

scissors

paper fastener

sewing needle

1 Trace different sized plates on painted cardboard, then cut the circles out.

2 Make a hole in the center of each with the needle. Bind together with the paper fastener.

3 Write letters and numbers, evenly spaced, around each circle with the silver and black pens.

Write a letter in code using your cipher disk.

Ask your friends to try to unravel the secret code

4 Take the wheels apart. Trim the edges of the outer wheel in a zig-zag pattern, and decorate with glitter glue.

Bind the wheels back together with the paper fastener.

5 Cut star shapes and glue to the inner wheel. Decorate with glitter.

15

Beautiful books

A handmade, textured book with cut-out windows and gold-leaf pages.

Some books have pictures in them or stories to tell. Other books explain facts or ideas. Books have not always looked as they do today. The first books were wood or clay tablets with writing carved into them.

Stories on scrolls

About 3,000 years ago, the Chinese made books by writing on long strips of bamboo. In ancient Egypt, people wrote books on a special kind of paper, called papyrus, which was made from the stems of a river plant. Later, the ancient Greeks and Romans made books out of parchment and **vellum**, which they made from animal skins.

Books by hand

Until the invention of the **printing press**, every book was copied by hand. Medieval **monks** worked for months to make just one book. The books had hand-painted pictures and beautiful decorations, and were called illuminated manuscripts. This way of making books was slow and expensive. In 1440, the printing press was invented and the first printed books appeared. Today, millions of books are printed all around the world. You buy printed books in bookstores and borrow them from the library. Books are hardcover or paperback, big or small, colorful or black and white.

Rag book

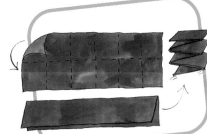

WHAT YOU NEED

large rectangular piece of black felt

bright and glittery fabric

needle

colored thread

scissors

wool

sequins

beads

glue

buttons

ribbons

1 Fold the black felt in half lengthwise and then back and forth to create pages. Ask an adult to iron the folds to make them sharp. Flatten out to show twelve pages.

Use different materials to design other rag books

2 Cut the colored fabric into various shapes and sizes, and glue onto the felt pages. Sew on beads and buttons and glue on sequins and other trimmings.

3 Fold up the finished book and sew on buttons and loops of ribbons for the fasteners.

Make a shooting star bookmark. Cut out two star shapes from felt. Place the ends of pieces of ribbon between the felt stars and glue the stars together. Decorate with beads and sequins.

Spinning disks

A circle of rainbows

Compact disks are made by burning tiny holes into a chemical spread over a plastic disk. The average music CD holds 74 minutes of music recorded as 3 billion holes. A strong light beam made by a laser shines on the spinning disk, and the bumps and holes, called pits and lands, are read and changed to sounds. When light shines on the disk, the pits bend the light, making a rainbow pattern.

CD-ROM

Disks hold more than just music. A CD contains three miles (5 km) of recording **track**, which makes it ideal for recording the long strings of information that computers need. Many **computer programs**, including games, are recorded on CDs. If you can read information on a CD but cannot add information to it, that type of CD is called a CD-ROM, which means Compact Disk–Read Only Memory.

To listen to music, your great-grandmother wound up a **gramophone** to play a **record**. Today, compact disks, or CDs, hold much more music than gramophone records and cassette tapes did. A cassette tape needs to be wound and rewound to find the song you want. A disk lets you find the song instantly. No wonder disks are the most popular way of storing music and information. Compact disks hold hundreds of songs, and play them back perfectly every time.

Minidisks and MP3

Minidisks are even smaller than CDs. A minidisk recorder fits into the palm of your hand. Minidisks cannot hold a lot of computer data, but they can hold 80 minutes of music. **Prerecorded** minidisks are like CDs, with pits and lands. Minidisks for home recording have a layer that becomes magnetized by lasers, allowing information to be stored on it. MP3 players are even smaller than minidisks. MP3 players have special **flash-memory chips** to record music from the **Internet**. An MP3 player smaller than a pen can hold two hours of stereo sound.

Communication

Musical notes

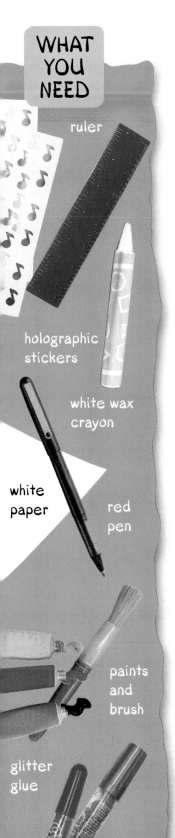

WHAT YOU NEED

holographic stickers

ruler

white wax crayon

white paper

red pen

paints and brush

glitter glue

1 Draw large treble and bass clefs in white wax crayon on white paper. Add some big musical notes.

2 Paint on a yellow and orange wash so that your clefs and notes show through.

3 Use a ruler to draw groups of five horizontal lines in red pen.

4 Stick metallic or holographic notes on the lines and in the spaces, so the music travels up and down the lines, or staves.

5 Stick on strips of holographic shapes to divide the music into sections.

Use glitter glue to make bar lines. Your melody is complete

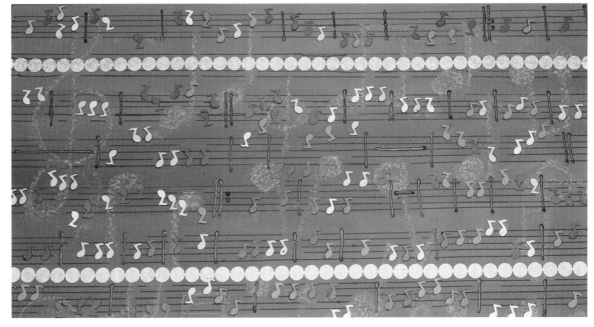

Newsprint

Newspapers deliver the news. They are important because they keep us up-to-date with what is going on in the world. As well as letting us know the daily news, they tell interesting stories and pass on useful information. Newspapers also let us know the latest score in a football game, and details of TV programs or movies. Some even print cartoons to make us laugh.

Latest!

The first printed daily newspaper was published in London, England, 300 years ago. Written news was around long before then! Handwritten sheets of paper were posted in public places for people to read in Rome in 59 B.C. These sheets were called Acta Diurna, which means Daily News. Today, most newspapers are published every day. Sometimes different editions, such as a morning edition, an afternoon edition, and an evening edition, are published through the day. Each edition tells the latest news. Some local newspapers only come out once a week. These papers usually just print news about the local area.

Hottest!

Reporters collect the news as it happens. Some stories are sent across the world by phone or the Internet. Photographs are used with the best stories. The editor of the newspaper decides which stories will appear in the paper, and which will be the top story, printed on the front page. As well as using eye-catching photographs to attract our attention, strong **headlines** must also be written! When the newspaper is ready, printing presses produce the thousands of copies that are then folded, packed, and sent to homes and stores. All this may happen overnight, so that you can wake up to the latest news in print.

Tabloids and broadsheets

Tabloid newspapers are usually small-sized and have more sports, gossip about celebrities, and photographs. Broadsheet newspapers are larger and usually print news stories in more detail. Both kinds of newspapers have advertisements, which help pay for the cost of producing the newspaper.

Newspaper man

WHAT YOU NEED

- small plastic bottle
- two styrofoam balls
- wire
- scissors
- masking tape
- glue
- toothpicks
- small piece of wood or styrofoam
- newspapers

Varnish your model with watered-down glue

1 Make two holes in the base of the bottle. Insert two long pieces of wire, and twist them to make legs. Cut a ball in half, and push it onto the wire legs for the feet.

Make a newspaper from clippings for your man to hold.

2 Make two arms with hands and long fingers using wire. Poke each arm through a hole in the body. Tape around the arms to keep them in place. Glue the model to a styrofoam or wood base.

3 Tape the second ball to the top of the bottle for the head. Wrap newspaper around part of a toothpick and jab it into the ball for the nose.

4 Glue strips of newspaper all over the model. Cut individual letters from newsprint to make eyes and a mouth. Cover the base with colorful newspaper photos.

Stamps and postmarks

It is exciting to get a letter in the mail, especially if it has traveled a long way across the world! You can tell if a letter has come from overseas by looking at the stamp. Every country in the world creates its own set of stamps.

The Penny Black

When we mail a letter or parcel, we buy postage stamps to stick on the outside. Stamps pay for the cost of delivery. The first postage stamp was used in Britain in 1840. It had a picture of Queen Victoria on it, and was named the Penny Black.

From runner to airmail

The first letters were carried by people on foot or horseback, and by stagecoaches or ships. A letter took months to arrive! Later, letters and parcels were delivered by trains, and airplanes carried airmail to faraway countries. Today, about a billion items are mailed across the world every day. Mail is collected, sorted, and delivered, often overnight. Delivery is made quicker by **zip codes**, or postal codes, that tell the mail carrier where to deliver them. Zip codes are now read by sorting machines at the post office. Stamps are labeled with postmarks, which tells you where and when the letter was mailed.

A collection of stamps from around the world.

Design-a-stamp

WHAT YOU NEED

white paper

pencil

ruler

paintbrush

gluestick

paints

used stamps

black paper

scissors and pinking shears

1 Choose a theme for your stamps, such as famous artists.

2 Draw a narrow border around the edge of the paper. In pencil, draw your designs inside the border. Paint in bright colors.

3 To make a collage stamp, sort used stamps into color groups and glue in an interesting design onto paper.

4 Draw the profile of a friend on black paper. Cut out and glue in the corner of each stamp.

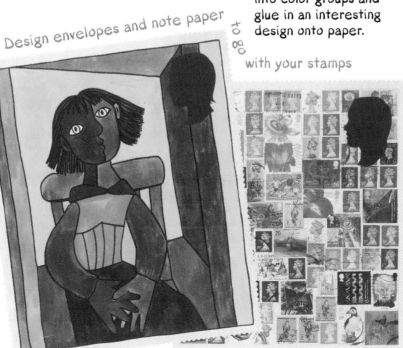

Design envelopes and note paper to go with your stamps

5 Finish by cutting around each stamp with pinking shears, or scissors with zigzag shaped blades.

Mount your stamps on colored poster board to make a display for your bedroom wall.

23

Body language

Did you know that you show your thoughts and feelings without speaking? You do this with your body language. Smiles and frowns, and the way you sit or stand are examples of body language. The way you look or move also sends out messages about how you feel.

Eyes down

It is easy to talk to someone who looks at you and nods, because this means they are listening. A person who crosses their arms and looks away is sending a signal to say they are not listening. Some people look down at the ground when they are being blamed for something. This often means they are sorry.

Watch your feet!

People from different places and cultures use body language in different ways. In some countries, it is rude to show the sole of your foot to someone, so be careful how you sit! Making a thumbs up sign means "good" in Europe and North America. Making the same sign in the Middle East is very rude!

Playing to the crowd

A mime is a story told through body movement, without words. Mime artists make us imagine there are other people and objects around them by the way they move. In a similar way, audiences can tell what dancers are feeling by the way they move to music.

Sign language

Languages for people with hearing difficulties combine mouthing the words and making hand and arm movements. Lipreading and following the movements make understanding as easy as listening.

Mime artists wear face paints to exaggerate facial expressions, and add drama to performances.

Communication

Theatrical masks

WHAT YOU NEED

gold and silver poster board

pencil

scissors

glue

sequins

glitter

glass beads

sewing needle

elastic

2 Draw patterns on the shiny side of each mask, then decorate with glitter and sequins.

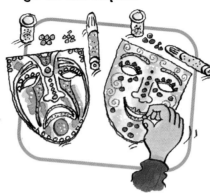

1 Draw outlines of masks on the poster board. Draw one mask with happy (comic) features, the other with a sad face (tragic). Cut them out.

3 Make a hole by the side of each eye with a needle. Thread elastic through the holes and tie a knot behind the mask. You can also make hand-held masks by gluing the faces onto sticks.

Decorate your tragedy mask in cold colors with bold patterns and shadows

Decorate your comedy mask in warm colors and swirly glitter patterns

25

Television

When you look at a television screen, your eyes are fooled into seeing many different colors. The colors are actually a mixture of tiny red, green, and blue dots! When the pictures change quickly, you think they are moving. In fact, the pictures on the screen are still. It is only because the **pixels** change so fast that you see a moving image.

The camera end

A television camera splits the light from a scene into red, green, and blue. The colors are then changed into a code of tiny electric signals, and linked with coded sound signals. The picture and sound are then **broadcast**, or sent out, through the air as **radio waves**.

The television end

A television set is a box with three color guns at one end and a glass screen at the other. The screen is coated inside with a special chemical called **phosphor**. When the guns fire tiny electric signals at the screen, the phosphor makes dots of red, green, or blue light, and the picture appears.

Bringing your picture

Not all of the pictures you see on television are broadcast from a studio. You may be seeing images that have been bounced across the world from a geostationary **satellite**. A geostationary satellite is fixed in space at a certain height so that it turns with the Earth. Your television program might also have traveled through underground cables.

Communication

Goggle-box

WHAT YOU NEED

bottle caps

cardboard box with lid

tracing paper

glue

tin foil

thread

paints and brush

scissors

silver pen

black paper

white paper

garland

acetate

pipe cleaners

1 Cut a rectangular hole in the bottom of the box for the TV screen. Cut the same sized hole in the lid for the light source. Paint both a bright color.

2 Cut out acetate for the screen, and tracing paper for the back of the TV. Glue in place behind the cut-out holes.

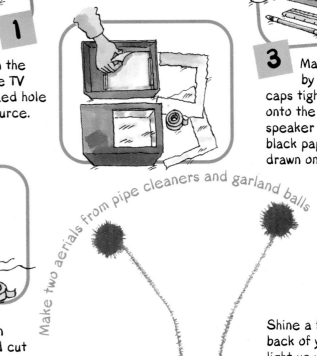

3 Make knobs and dials by covering the bottle caps tightly with foil. Glue onto the box. Make a speaker from a rectangle of black paper with a grid drawn on it in silver pen.

4 Draw a scene on paper. Color and cut out the parts of the picture separately. Attach two pieces of thread to each picture. Take the lid off the box and glue or tape the thread to the inside top of the box at different distances from the screen to create a 3-D effect.

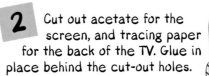

Make two aerials from pipe cleaners and garland balls

Shine a flashlight at the back of your goggle-box to light up your image.

27

Computerland

Can you really believe what you see? When you watch a movie or a television program, you might see a world entirely created by a computer. Recent films have starred **computer-generated** actors, or placed real actors in virtual worlds, such as dinosaur habitats or the Colosseum in ancient Rome. Computer games let you interact with imaginary worlds. Virtual reality, or VR, goes one step further by placing us in **cyberspace**.

Digital dots

Pictures are drawn on the computer as dots and every dot is given a number. This is called **digitizing**. Once you have digitized pictures and sounds, you can change them any way you like, and make almost anything happen.

Computer games

When you play a computer game, you are watching a computer graphic, or image. The graphics refresh, or change, so fast that thay appear to move. By moving and clicking a computer mouse or moving a joystick, you control the game.

Virtual reality

Using today's computer technology, you can enter a different world. Virtual reality takes you into cyberspace, an imaginary world. VR goggles project a 3-D picture of cyberspace for you, and stereo headphones add the sound. A special glove records every movement of your hand, so that you can interact with this virtual world. Lift your arm and VR technology responds. Whole-body VR suits make cyberspace even more realistic.

With these virtual reality goggles, you can escape into a computer-generated world.

Crazy computer

cardboard boxes and tube

silver and red foil

bottle caps

sequins

metallic paper

wire

two corks

small plastic containers with lids

tape

scissors

silver and black poster board

glue

paper

paper mesh

1 Wrap four boxes in foil. Seal the ends with glue or tape.

2 Coil wire by wrapping it around the tube. Glue on sequins and push wire ends into the corks. Glue the corks onto the biggest box for antennae.

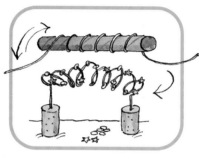

3 Glue pieces of black paper and a sequin in the center of two plastic lids for the movie reels. Glue onto the front of the big box.

4 Make a printer and a power unit from smaller boxes. Decorate with foil knobs, metallic frames, mesh, and sequins.

Make a glitzy control panel! Wrap foil around bottle caps for knobs. Make dials from plastic lids, paper, and sequins.

Make flashing red lights from foil-covered bottle caps

Wired up

Telephones turn sounds into electrical signals, and these signals are carried on copper wires from your home to the telephone exchange. Here the signals are sent through **optical fibers** to the person you are calling. Their telephone turns the message back into sound. On the way, the message may travel across the country, under the sea, or be bounced from a satellite in space.

Making connections

When there were very few telephones, people called an operator and told them who they wanted to speak to. The operator pulled and pushed plugs on the telephone switchboard to put the call through. Now, with millions of calls every minute, the calls are connected automatically.

Handy mobiles

You do not need to stand still to make a phone call. Mobile phones, or cell phones, send a signal that is picked up by a base station. Most countries are divided into areas called cells, and each cell has a base station. Wherever you are calling from, you are in one of these cells, and a base station is nearby. The base station puts your call on the telephone **network**, and your friend, standing in another cell near a base station far away, hears the signal sent to their mobile phone.

Pictures by phone

Telephone lines carry more than voices. They also carry documents, sent by a facsimile machine, or fax, that changes an image into a code. The fax machine scans the document, then it sends it to another fax that prints it out in words and pictures. Telephone lines can also carry messages between computers – in pictures, words, and sounds.

Funky phones

two small plastic containers

fake fur

pen

colored felt

beads and sequins

feather trim

sewing needle

scissors or pinking shears

strong glue

thick string or wool

1 Cut two rectangles of fur long enough to wrap around each plastic container and glue in place.

2 Use the pen to trace around the bottoms of the containers on felt. Cut out the two circles with zigzag scissors. Glue onto the bottoms.

3 Cut noses from pink felt. Make eyes using circles of black and white felt with sequins and beads in the middle. Glue on.

4 Glue semi-circles of black and pink felt together for the ears. Fold the sides in as shown. Glue the ears to the rims of the plastic containers.

Use your phone to talk to a friend

To use your phone, face a friend and pull the string tight between you. Hold a phone to your ear while your friend talks clearly into the other one. Their voice will pass along the string as vibrations.

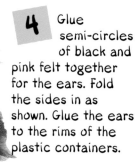

5 Make hair by gluing on feather trim. Pierce the base of each container with the sewing needle. Thread the string through both containers and tie a knot on the inside.

On the Web

All over the world, millions of computers in homes, schools, and offices are connected to the Internet. The Internet lets people explore the World Wide Web, which we shorten to www, and to keep in contact with each other by e-mail.

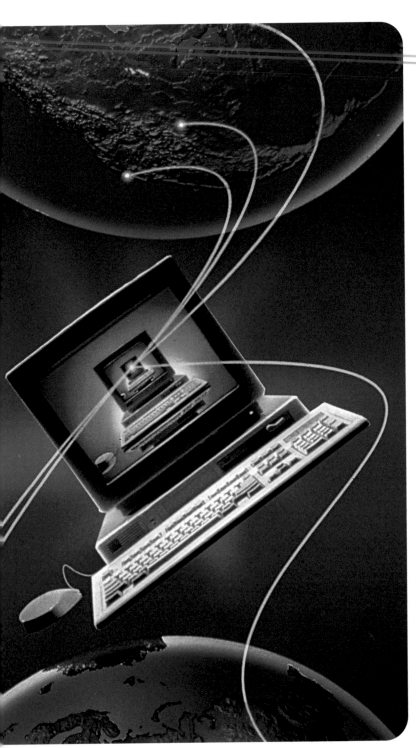

Global network

The Internet is an international network of computers that talk to each other by cables, telephone wires, and radio signals. The Internet began in the USA in 1969, as a Department of Defense computer network called ARPANET. Researchers outside of the military also began to use it. By the mid 1990s, the Internet was available to everyone with a computer.

Giant encyclopedia

The World Wide Web is part of the Internet. It is a giant encyclopedia, containing text, pictures, sound, and video. If you need information in a hurry, the Web is often the best place to look. The Web was invented in 1989 by Tim Berners-Lee. He invented a code called Hypertext Markup Language, or HTML. HTML allows items in separate documents, or even on different computers, to be linked.

Surfing the net

You can explore the Web or "surf the net" by using a computer program called a **browser**. Then you can use a **search engine** to look for information on any subject that interests you. Or you can hop from one subject to another – just for fun!

Communication

Weave a web

Create a unique and personal web site

WHAT YOU NEED

WHAT
YOU
NEED

feathers

string

bamboo
sticks

gold or silver
spray paint

beads and
sequins

scissors

ribbon

strong
glue

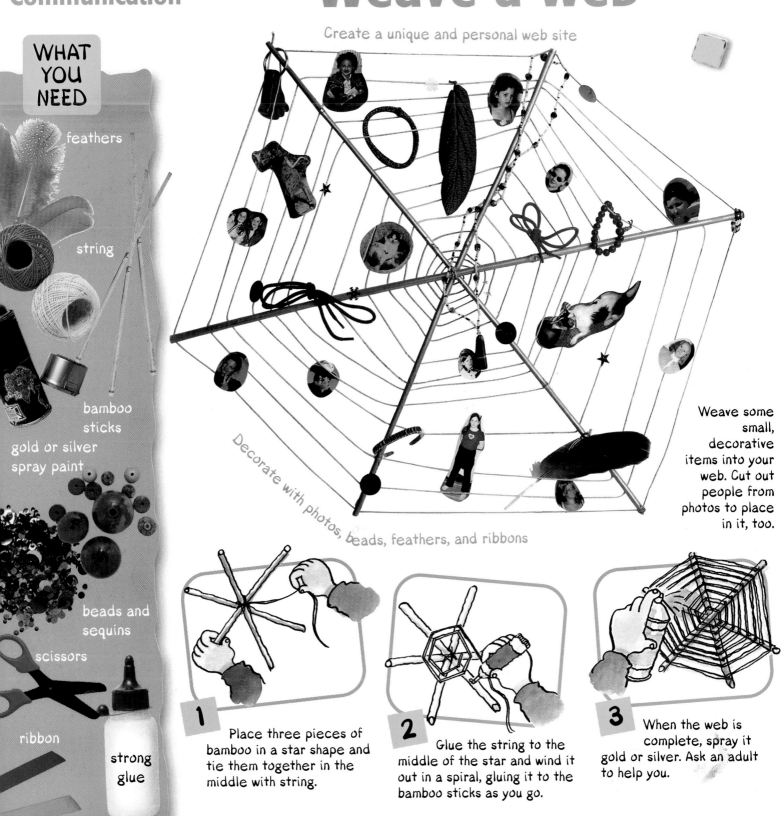

Decorate with photos, beads, feathers, and ribbons

Weave some small, decorative items into your web. Cut out people from photos to place in it, too.

1 Place three pieces of bamboo in a star shape and tie them together in the middle with string.

2 Glue the string to the middle of the star and wind it out in a spiral, gluing it to the bamboo sticks as you go.

3 When the web is complete, spray it gold or silver. Ask an adult to help you.

Satellite signals

A photograph of Earth at night taken by a satellite.

Today, there are hundreds of satellites whirling around the Earth, doing important work for people on the ground. Satellite pictures show an amazing view of the world below.

Artificial satellites

A satellite is a machine designed to travel in space. It travels around, or orbits, Earth. Each satellite has a small motor to keep it at the correct height and in the correct orbit. A ground control center tracks the satellite and sends it orders.

Spy and scientific satellites

Spy satellites are used by governments and military forces. These satellites check the weapons, armies, and military bases of other countries. Scientific satellites do a wide range of work. The Landsat is a satellite that studies Earth, showing where oil and minerals might be found.

Communications satellites

We use communications satellites every day without knowing it! Satellites such as the Comstar and Intelsat send television signals around the world. They also send millions of telephone calls, many of which contain information being sent on the Internet.

Silver satellite

1 Cover a large box with foil and a smaller one with silver paper. Decorate both with squares, triangles, and stripes of holographic paper. Glue the small box on top of the larger box.

Make a small satellite dish from glittery pipe cleaners.

2 Pierce a hole in both ends of the large box to hold a wooden stick.

3 Cut a section from one of the pie plates as shown, and glue to form a cone shape for the large dish. Push over the end of the stick and tape in place. Use bottle caps for decoration.

Decorate bottle caps, and attach to your box to make boosters

4 Make the wing by piercing the box through the sides with another stick. Glue holographic strips over both sides of the stick to form rotating panels.

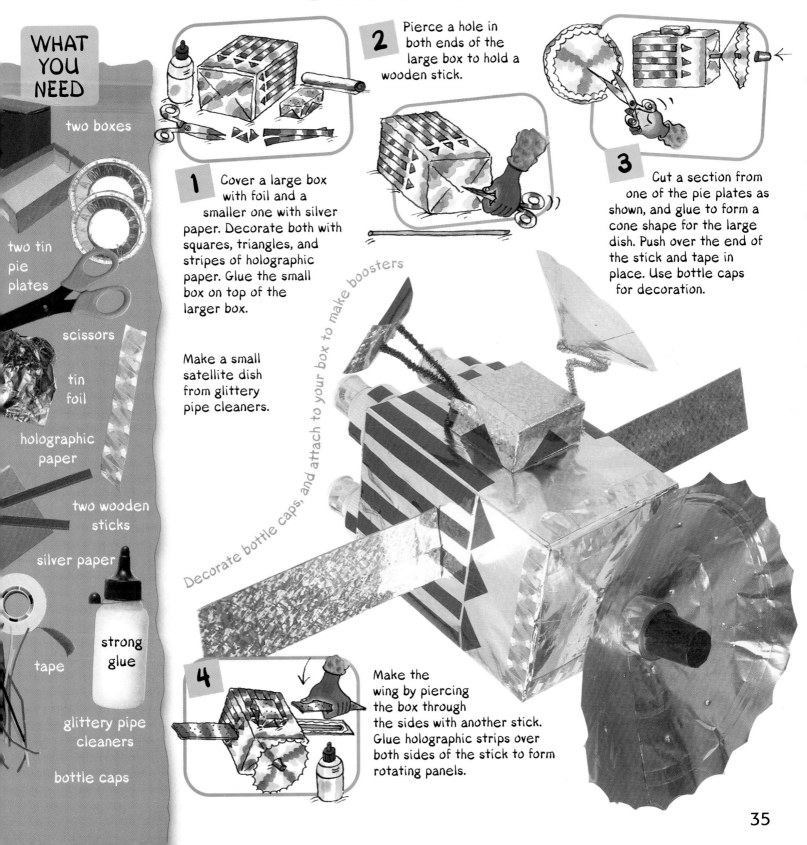

Microchips

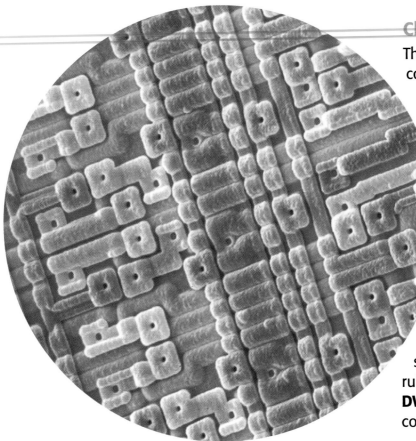

The magnified surfaces of a silicon chip (above) and a microprocessor chip (right).

The first computers were so big, you could walk around inside them. In 1959, tiny patches of a chemical called silicon were linked by metal tracks, replacing the biggest parts of earlier computers. In 1971, the first computer chip was made, which put all the memory and calculating power onto a tiny scrap of silicon. This first chip had 2,300 patches of silicon on it. By 1999, the average chip had 10 million patches of silicon.

Chips and PCs

The invention of the **microchip** made small personal computers, or PCs, possible. Large storage spaces for information and calculating power were put into a tiny box. Modern computers do a billion different things every second. The Central Processing Unit, or CPU, contains so many fast-working chips that it gets hot and needs a fan to cool it down.

RAM and ROM

Computers have two types of memory. **RAM** is Random Access Memory. RAM chips are used to store the programs and data you use. RAM chips change the picture as you play a computer game. **ROM**, or Read Only Memory, stores the game itself, including the instructions and rules. Computer games are usually on a CD-ROM or a **DVD-ROM**, which you put into your computer before you play.

Computer mice

When you use a computer, your mouse changes your hand movements into electrical signals. Operating the mouse moves a cursor, or pointer, on the screen. Pressing a button on the mouse sends instructions to the computer.

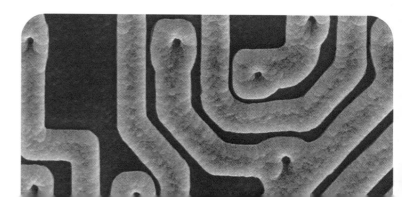

Communication

Circuit board

WHAT YOU NEED

green paper

scissors

colored paper

glue

small plastic tubes

corrugated cardboard

craft wire

assorted boxes and cartons

pencil

1 Make a base board by gluing green paper to the corrugated cardboard.

2 Arrange the boxes and plastic tubes on the board. These will be the microchips and resistors. Draw around them to mark their positions.

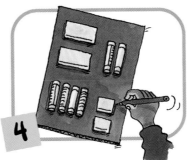

4 Cover the microchip boxes in colored paper, decorate and glue in position.

3 To make the resistors, cover the tubes and decorate with strips of colored paper of various widths. Ask an adult to make holes in the base board. Attach wire to the resistors, then thread it through the holes. Twist the ends of the wires together.

Cut strips of colored paper to connect all the components on your board

Amazing ads

Advertisements, or ads, are everywhere. We see them on TV, at the movies, on the Internet, in magazines, and in the street. Advertisements are there to grab our attention, to change the way we think, and to try to make us buy something! The bigger and brighter the ads, the more likely they are to make an impact and catch our eye.

Face the facts

An advertisement tells you important facts about products such as breakfast cereals or the latest computer games. You usually see a picture of the product, and its special features are pointed out in a catchy phrase called a slogan. The slogan might say that something is tasty, healthy, long-lasting, or even good-looking! The idea is to make a product sound so good that people will want to buy it.

Hidden meanings

Many modern advertisements contain hidden messages, so we do not always know what is being advertised. You have to look carefully to find out what the company is advertising. If a television commercial makes you watch and wonder, you are more likely to remember it.

Brand names

The shapes, colors, and words of different **brands** of goods are carefully protected from being copied. A popular brand name is very valuable. Some soft drink brands are worth billions of dollars. Manufacturers of sports clothes make their brand labels or logos so famous that words are not needed on running shoes and baseball caps. Brand thieves, called pirates, try to copy products. This is illegal and manufacturers spend millions of dollars protecting their brands.

A street in Tokyo lit up by hundreds of advertising signs.

Magnetic billboard

WHAT YOU NEED

poster board

black pen

glue

pencil crayons

scissors

tin foil

small magnets

garland

baking tray

ribbon or gold thread

1

Draw a variety of food ads with wacky background shapes, and color them in.

2 Cut around each image and glue a magnet to the back.

3 Make a magnet board from the baking tray. Place it face down and glue a sheet of tin foil to the surface. Glue garland to the edges to decorate.

Make up some of your own brand logos and slogans

4 Glue a piece of ribbon or gold thread to the back of the tray to hang it up. Arrange your magnet ads on the billboard.

Keypads and gadgets

Today, you can phone home, play a computer game, or write a text message from wherever you are. This is possible because gadgets are getting smaller and smaller. They are shrinking in size every few months, and becoming more powerful.

Pocket pals

The palm top computer is small enough to fit into your pocket but is very powerful. It can be used to keep your diary and to send messages to friends. **Infra-red beams** send your message to another palm top, and it can even read your handwriting! You can also carry a miniature television in your pocket. The latest models have a tiny screen that mixes red, blue, and green light to create the picture.

Throw-away phones

Mobile phones are also getting smaller. The first mobile phones were as big as a brick. Today's models are the size of a small candy bar. As well as telephone calls and text messages, the phones can receive faxes and access the Internet. All this is possible because the information is digitized using a string of instructions. The same string can carry two or more messages. This system is called multiplexing, and it allows you to access the Internet while making a telephone call. An American company recently developed a disposable mobile phone. It is made of special paper, and instead of wires it uses ink that conducts electricity. You buy it, use it, and then throw it away! Wristwatch phones are also being developed. Many companies already use wristwatch **beepers** so they can keep in touch with their employees when they are away from the office.

Large keyboards are mainly used in offices and homes. When people travel, they take smaller pocket-sized keypads.

Screen saver picture

old magazines

pencil

scissors

gluestick

graph paper

tracing paper

ruler

1 Choose a simple subject for your collage from a photo or picture with a lot of different colors. Copy the picture onto graph paper, using tracing paper if necessary.

2 Find pictures in magazines with the colors you need. Draw a square grid, and cut along the lines to make half-inch (1 cm) squares.

3 Work on one area at a time. Glue the square pieces onto your picture using shades of your chosen color. As you go along, stand back from your collage to make sure you can see the picture clearly.

Add shiny paper squares for a dazzling effect

41

Animatronics

Remote control

Animatronic creations are often used for close up shots in movies or for scenes where a remote-controlled model has to do something life-like, such as eating grass or swimming in the sea. These movie shots are linked with computer-generated scenes to make the character come to life.

Computerized images

Computer-generated imagery, or CGI, makes it possible to make movies without using live actors. A dinosaur model, scanned by laser and changed by a computer into thousands of tiny parts, can be moved into life-like positions on screen. An artist takes great care to make the dinosaur look as realistic as possible so that the character comes to life. Actors are also combined with CGI. For example, actors dressed as gladiators can battle in a scene from ancient Rome that only exists on the computer screen.

Animatronics is a way of making models or robots move realistically. A complicated network of wires carry **electronic** messages to electric motors that make eyes swivel, arms move, and fingers grip. Animatronic models and robots can make museum visits exciting or add to the fun at amusement parks.

Stop-action

Flexible models can be made and then filmed, frame by frame, or picture by picture, to look as though they are moving. A Plasticine model has to be moved 25 times to make one second of **animated** film. A full-length animated film consists of thousands of still frames of the models or drawings, which together create a moving picture.

Communication  Stroboscope!

WHAT YOU NEED

- black poster board
- white poster board
- glitter glue
- sequins
- scissors
- markers
- cork
- tracing paper
- plate
- sewing pin
- pad of paper
- pencil
- black pen
- two small beads

1 Draw around a plate and cut out the circle from the white poster board. Using a compass, draw a small circle inside the big circle.

2 Divide the outer part of the circle into twelve equal segments and cut out twelve triangular slits between them.

3

In the spaces that are left, draw twelve identical boxes, using tracing paper to reproduce them. Add a clown popping out of the box, showing more of his face each time. Draw a spiral in the middle of the disk. Color in the spiral.

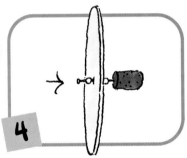

4 Poke a pin through the center of the disk. Put a bead on each side of the pin. Push a cork onto the free end on the underside of the disk.

Flipbook

1. Draw a stick figure to be the main character of your story. Plan a series of ten action pictures with a simple background.
2. Draw the first picture on page one. Turn over and repeat the picture, making small changes to the figure's actions.
3. When you get to the last picture, remove any blank pages.
4. Make a book cover using black poster board, glitter glue, and sequins.

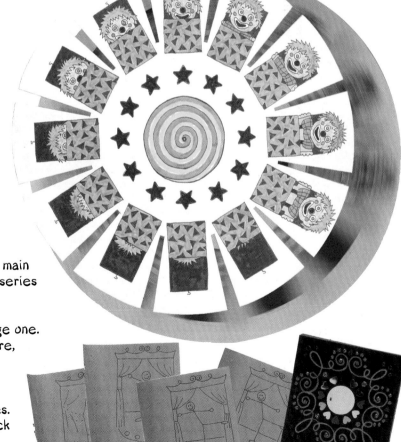

Animal chat

Have you ever watched two dogs greet each other? They sniff each other and sometimes wag their tails. If one dog feels threatened, its ears move back and it may even growl. It is telling the other dog to watch out! Although animals do not actually speak to each other, they do communicate in all kinds of ways.

Sign language

Humans use their faces to signal their feelings, and our nearest relatives, chimpanzees, also use their facial expressions to communicate. Humans have even been able to train chimpanzees to learn sign language. One chimp, named Washoe, learned to use 150 signs, and to understand 300. Honeybees use a type of sign language to communicate. Certain movements show the direction, distance, and size of **nectar** and **pollen** stores.

In touch

Elephants communicate with each other by making deep sounds. Howler monkeys scream at one another from the treetops. Animals also send messages with scents. A dog lifting its leg at every lamp post is marking its **territory**. The feathery **antennae** of a male moth can pick up the scent of a female moth a long way away.

Whale noise

Whales and dolphins are very intelligent animals that communicate by making sounds. Some whales make noises called songs to attract a mate. They also make chirps, screams, whistles, clicks, and grunts! Dolphins use combinations of whistles, squeaks, and clicks to communicate.

Communication

Musical turtles

1 Wrap the pebble in clear food wrap. Roll a ball of clay larger than the pebble, and push your thumb into the middle. Place the pebble into the hole and push the clay over the end to seal. Roll to make a smooth surface.

2 Let the clay partly dry overnight. Cut a line around the middle of the clay with the knife, as shown. Make holes in the top with the stick and another in the end for the mouthpiece.

3 Pull the two halves apart and remove the pebble and food wrap. Stick the turtle back together with wet clay.

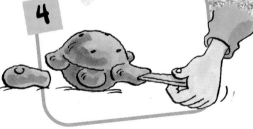

4 Make a head and legs from small balls of clay. Stick another ball over the mouthpiece and open with a flat stick.

5 Leave to dry for two days, then decorate with black marker.

Blow into the mouthpiece and cover the holes with your fingers

45

Glossary

abacus A calculating device made of a frame, wooden or wire rows, and beads.

animated In film-making, animation is the technique of shooting a series of drawings to look as if they were moving.

animatronics Animation techniques used to make models and robots move.

antenna A pair of feelers on the head of an insect.

Babylonians The people from the ancient civilization of Babylonia (3600 B.C. - 539 B.C.), in present-day Iraq.

bar code A code of black and white lines used to electronically identify many products we buy.

beeper An electronic device people wear or carry that beeps to tell them they have a message. It is also called a pager.

brand A symbol or name put on goods of a particular company.

broadcast To send out speech, music, pictures or other information by radio or TV.

browser A computer program used to find and display information on the Internet.

cipher disk A tool used to decipher codes.

communication Passing on and receiving information.

computer-generated Produced by a computer.

computer program The set of instructions that makes a computer work in a specific way.

cyberspace The world of information that only exists within computers.

digitizing Storing information as a string of numbers.

DVD-ROM Digital Video Disc - Read Only Memory.

electronic Information created and carried by electrical pulses.

e-mail Electronic mail, a way of sending and receiving messages through the Internet.

emblem An object or picture of an object that represents or identifies something else.

flash-memory chips Small computer chips that are used to store information in devices such as M3P players and cameras. These chips keep the information after the device is turned off, without having to save to a disk.

gramophone An old-fashioned machine for playing records.

headlines The titles of newspaper stories that are set in bigger type.

Infra-red beam A ray of light energy that humans cannot see.

Internet The international network of computers which allows people to access information on the World Wide Web.

Mayan The people of an ancient civilization (1500 B.C. - 1500 A.D.) of Central America.

microchip A tiny electric circuit on a piece of silicon on which information can be stored.

Middle Ages The period of history in Europe from about 500 A.D to 1500. Medieval is a word used to describe this time.

monks Men who devote their lives to a religion. Monks in medieval times were also scribes who copied books and kept records.

nectar A sweet liquid found in some flowers. Bees collect nectar to make honey.

network A group of computers or other electronic devices that are linked, allowing users to share information.

optical fibers Fine glass strands that carry signals as electrical pulses.

phosphor A chemical used in television receivers that is very light sensitive.

pixel A small dot of digitized information.

pollen Tiny yellow grains that fertilize female cells of a plant to produce seeds.

prerecorded Recorded at an earlier time.

printing press A machine used to print the pages of a book.

private key The half of a public key, or system for deciphering a code, that is known only to the user.

public key A code system in which the key to making the code is different from the key for deciphering the code.

radio waves Part of a large spectrum of waves known as electromagnetic waves. We cannot see radio waves.

RAM Random Access Memory is part of a computer's memory where information is stored.

ROM Read Only Memory is the part of the computer's memory where information can be read but not changed or deleted.

record A thin piece of plastic, usually vinyl, that has grooves on the surface for recording sound.

satellite An object circling the Earth.

search engine A computer program that allows you to look up information on the Internet.

tablet A flat piece of wood, stone, or clay used for writing on.

territory The area that an animal chooses as its own.

track A section or path of a magnetic tape, record, or disk, on which information is recorded.

vellum An animal skin stretched and flattened to form a sheet for writing on.

zip code Numbers assigned to delivery areas in the United States. In Canada, letters and numbers are used and called postal codes.

Index

Materials guide

WHAT YOU NEED

gold foil

silver foil

filler paste

PVA glue

flour

salt

cellophane or acetate

The crafts in this book require the use of materials and products that are easily purchased in craft stores. If you cannot locate some materials, you can substitute other materials with those we have listed here, or use your imagination to make the craft with what you have on hand.

Gold foil: can be found in craft stores. It is very delicate and sometimes tears.

Silver foil: can be found in craft stores. It is very delicate, soft and sometimes tears. For some crafts, tin or aluminum foil can be substituted. Aluminum foil is a less delicate material and makes a harder finished craft.

PVA glue: commonly called polyvinyl acetate. It is a modeling glue that creates a type of varnish when mixed with water. It is also used as a strong glue. In some crafts, other strong glues can be substituted, and used as an adhesive, but not as a varnish.

Filler paste: sometimes called plaster of Paris. It is a paste that hardens when it dries. It can be purchased at craft and hardware stores.

Paste: a paste of 1/2 cup flour, one tablespoon of salt and one cup of warm water can be made to paste strips of newspaper as in a papier mâché craft. Alternatively, wallpaper paste can be purchased and mixed as per directions on the package.

Cellophane: a clear or colored plastic material. Acetate can also be used in crafts that call for this material. Acetate is a clear, or colored, thin plastic that can be found in craft stores.

1 2 3 4 5 6 7 8 9 0   Printed in the USA   0 9 8 7 6 5 4 3 2